MESSAGES
FROM THE
Unicorns
COLORING BOOK

MESSAGES
FROM THE

Unicorns
COLORING BOOK

DOREEN VIRTUE

Illustrations by Heather Luciana

HAY HOUSE

Carlsbad, California • New York City • London
Sydney •Johannesburg • Vancouver • New Delhi

♡ Rock
4 March 2017

Tradepaper ISBN: 978-1-4019-5289-1

10 9 8 7 6 5 4 3 2 1
1st edition, November 2016

Printed in the United States of America

There's a reason why every major museum displays paintings and tapestries that feature Unicorns: these magnificent animals were real, physical, living beings at one time. Instead of becoming extinct, the Unicorns raised their energy so that they are now spiritual beings.

Children and highly creative people naturally gravitate toward Unicorns because they can sense their pure, healing energy. In fact, inviting Unicorns into your life can help you to unleash your natural creativity.

To take you to the magical world of the unicorns and help you connect deeply with their energy, I've created a guided meditation and also a selection of enchanting, high-vibrational music to help quiet your mind as you color. You'll find details of how to access this bonus content at the back of the book.

I highly recommend using nontoxic and fair trade coloring pencils, as the Unicorns care deeply about healing and preserving the environment. Let your imagination go wild with the colors you use. After all, Unicorns are associated with all the bright and sparkly colors of the rainbow!

Each message that accompanies the illustrations is a genuine message from the spirit of the Unicorns, because they wish to connect with and help you in any way they can.

Love, Doreen

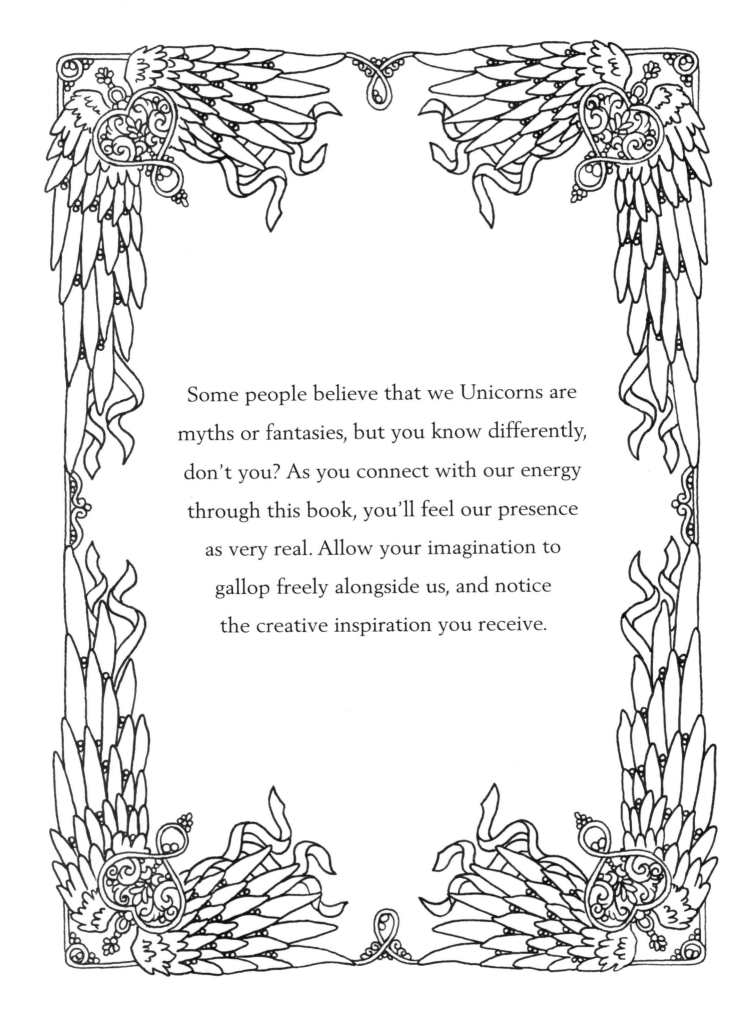

Some people believe that we Unicorns are myths or fantasies, but you know differently, don't you? As you connect with our energy through this book, you'll feel our presence as very real. Allow your imagination to gallop freely alongside us, and notice the creative inspiration you receive.

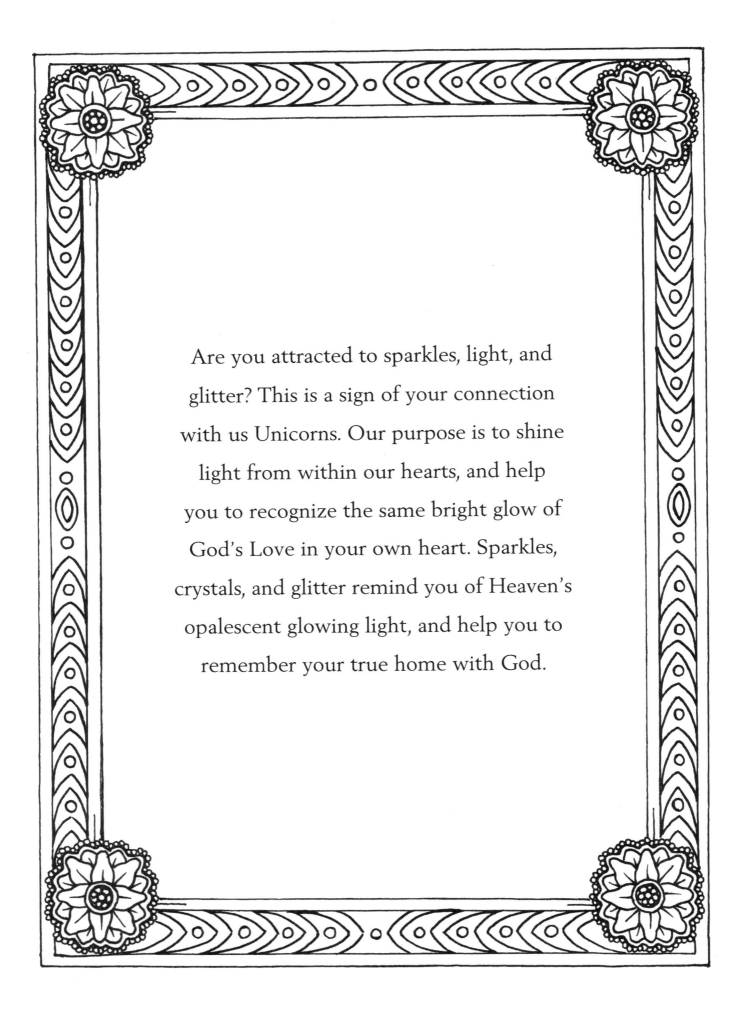

Are you attracted to sparkles, light, and glitter? This is a sign of your connection with us Unicorns. Our purpose is to shine light from within our hearts, and help you to recognize the same bright glow of God's Love in your own heart. Sparkles, crystals, and glitter remind you of Heaven's opalescent glowing light, and help you to remember your true home with God.

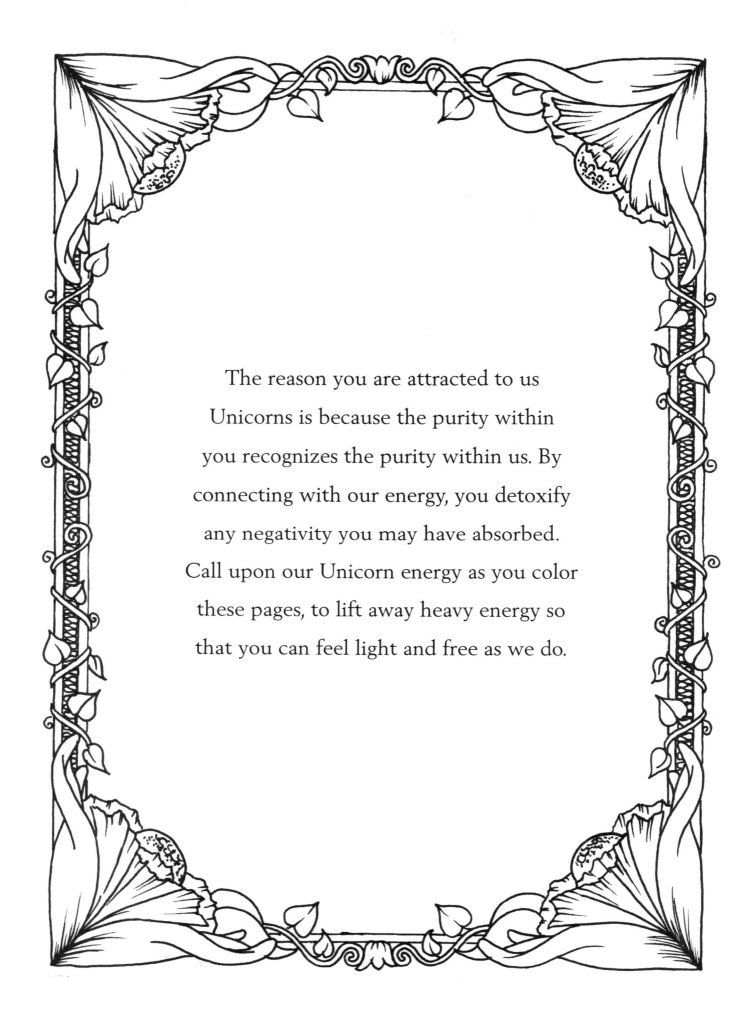

The reason you are attracted to us
Unicorns is because the purity within
you recognizes the purity within us. By
connecting with our energy, you detoxify
any negativity you may have absorbed.
Call upon our Unicorn energy as you color
these pages, to lift away heavy energy so
that you can feel light and free as we do.

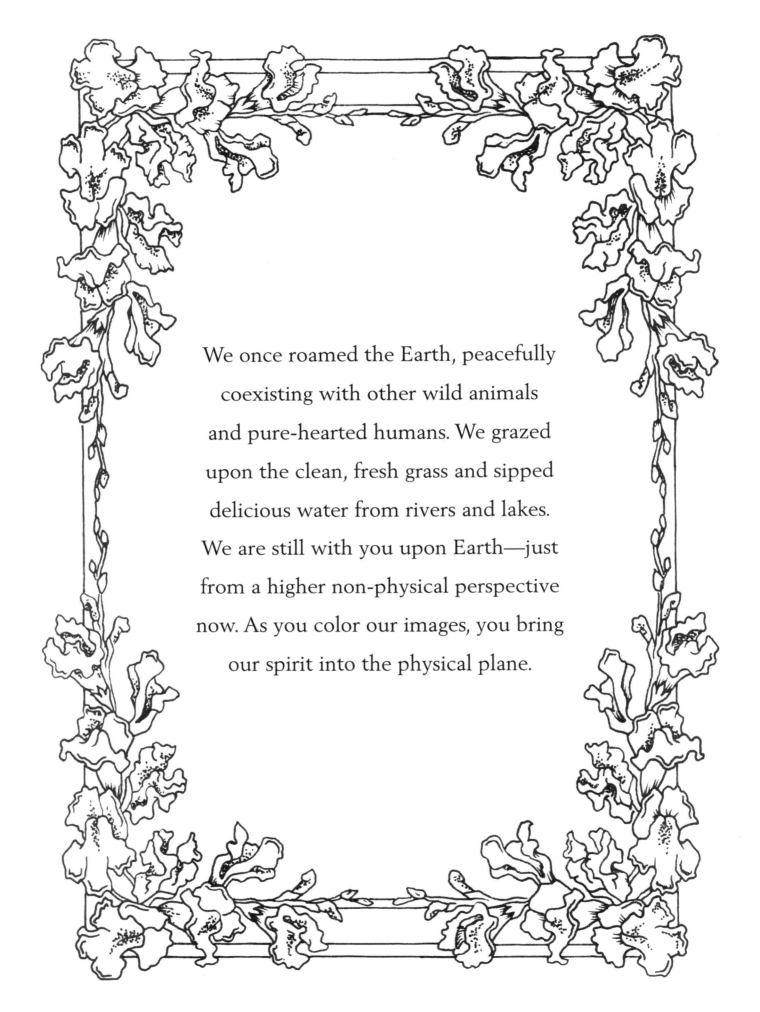

We once roamed the Earth, peacefully coexisting with other wild animals and pure-hearted humans. We grazed upon the clean, fresh grass and sipped delicious water from rivers and lakes. We are still with you upon Earth—just from a higher non-physical perspective now. As you color our images, you bring our spirit into the physical plane.

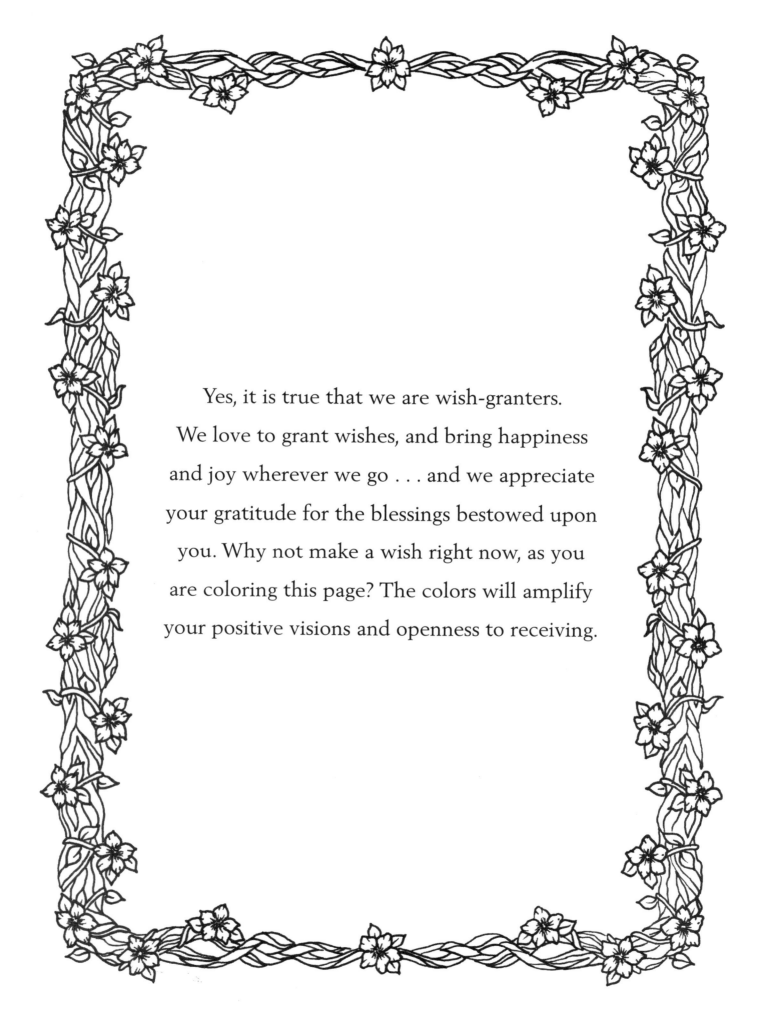

Yes, it is true that we are wish-granters. We love to grant wishes, and bring happiness and joy wherever we go . . . and we appreciate your gratitude for the blessings bestowed upon you. Why not make a wish right now, as you are coloring this page? The colors will amplify your positive visions and openness to receiving.

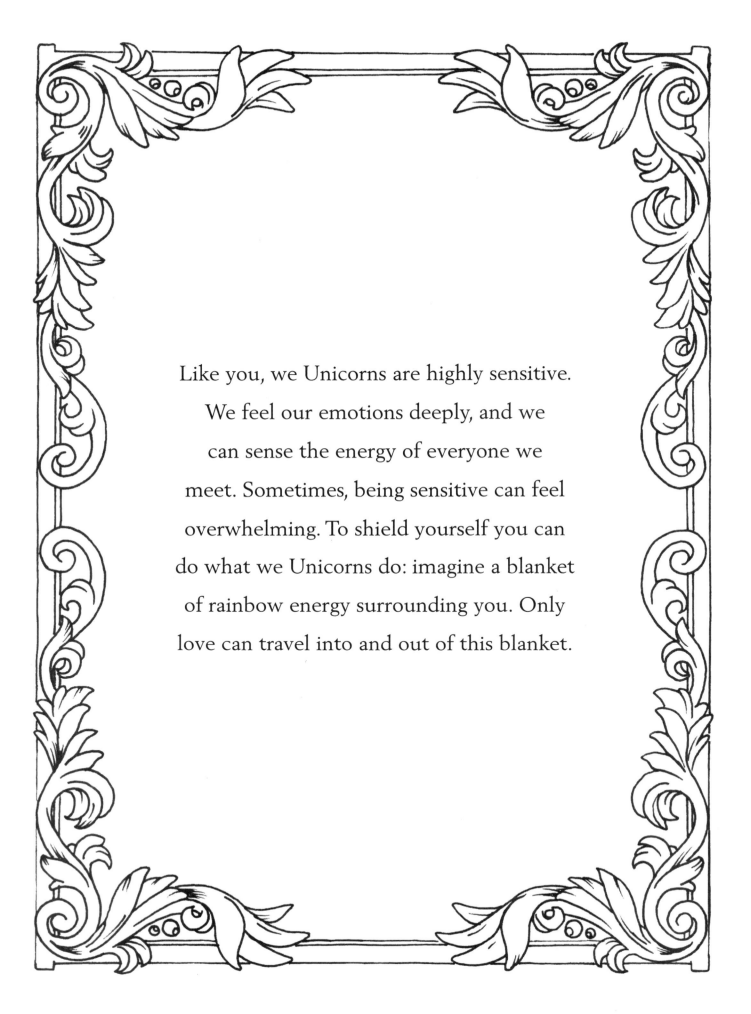

Like you, we Unicorns are highly sensitive.
We feel our emotions deeply, and we
can sense the energy of everyone we
meet. Sometimes, being sensitive can feel
overwhelming. To shield yourself you can
do what we Unicorns do: imagine a blanket
of rainbow energy surrounding you. Only
love can travel into and out of this blanket.

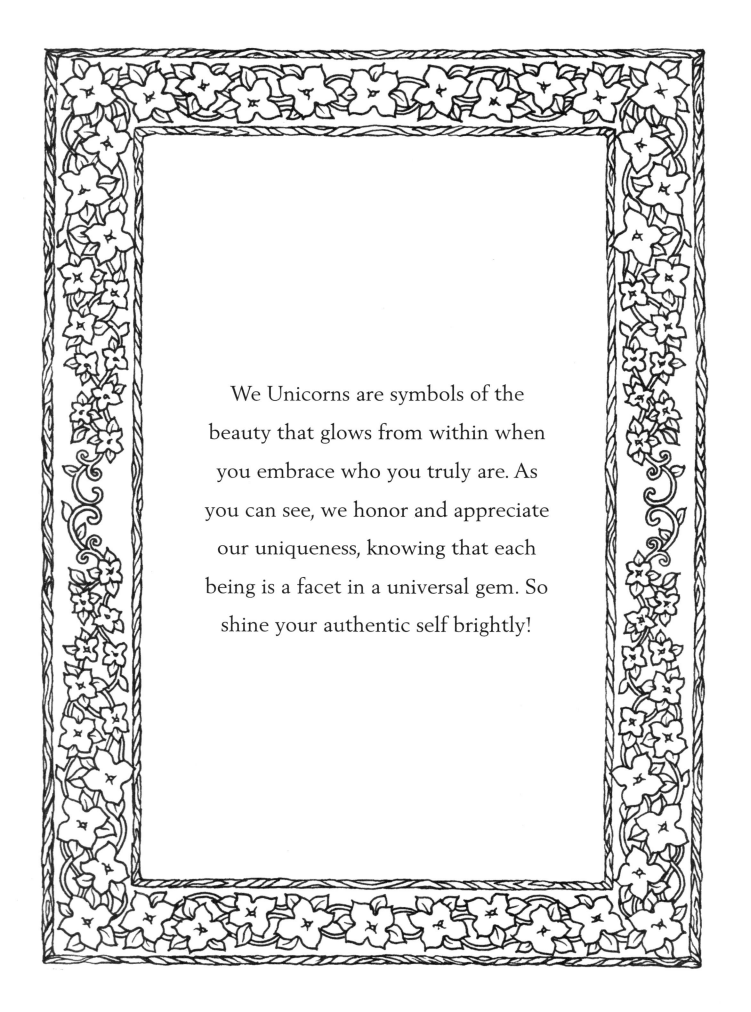

We Unicorns are symbols of the beauty that glows from within when you embrace who you truly are. As you can see, we honor and appreciate our uniqueness, knowing that each being is a facet in a universal gem. So shine your authentic self brightly!

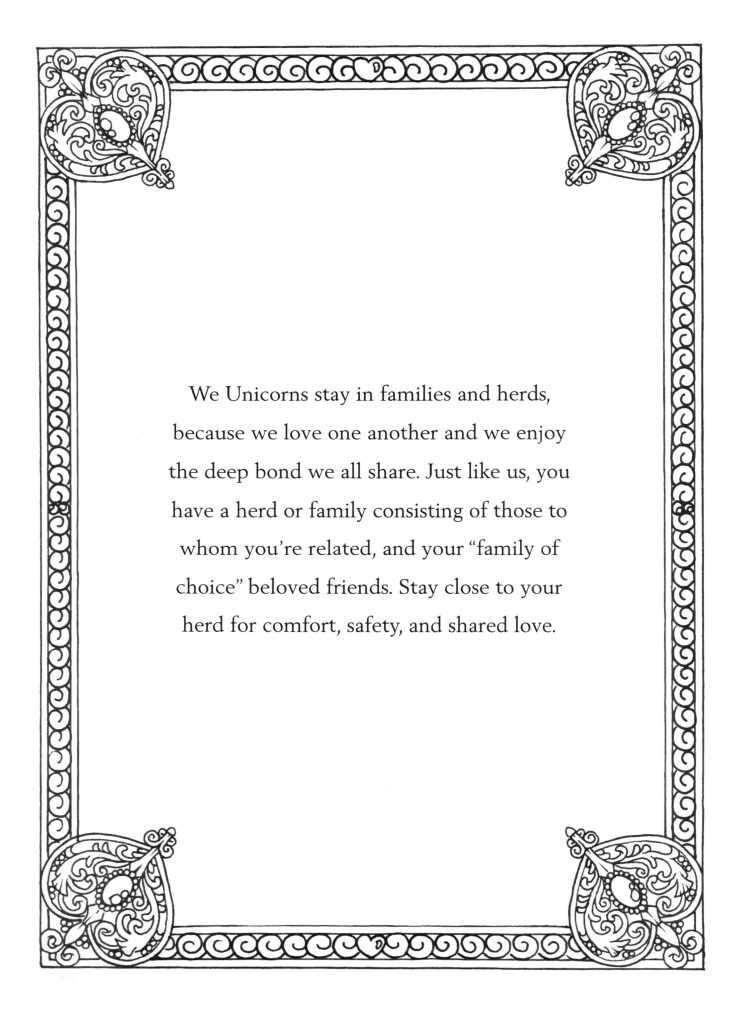

We Unicorns stay in families and herds, because we love one another and we enjoy the deep bond we all share. Just like us, you have a herd or family consisting of those to whom you're related, and your "family of choice" beloved friends. Stay close to your herd for comfort, safety, and shared love.

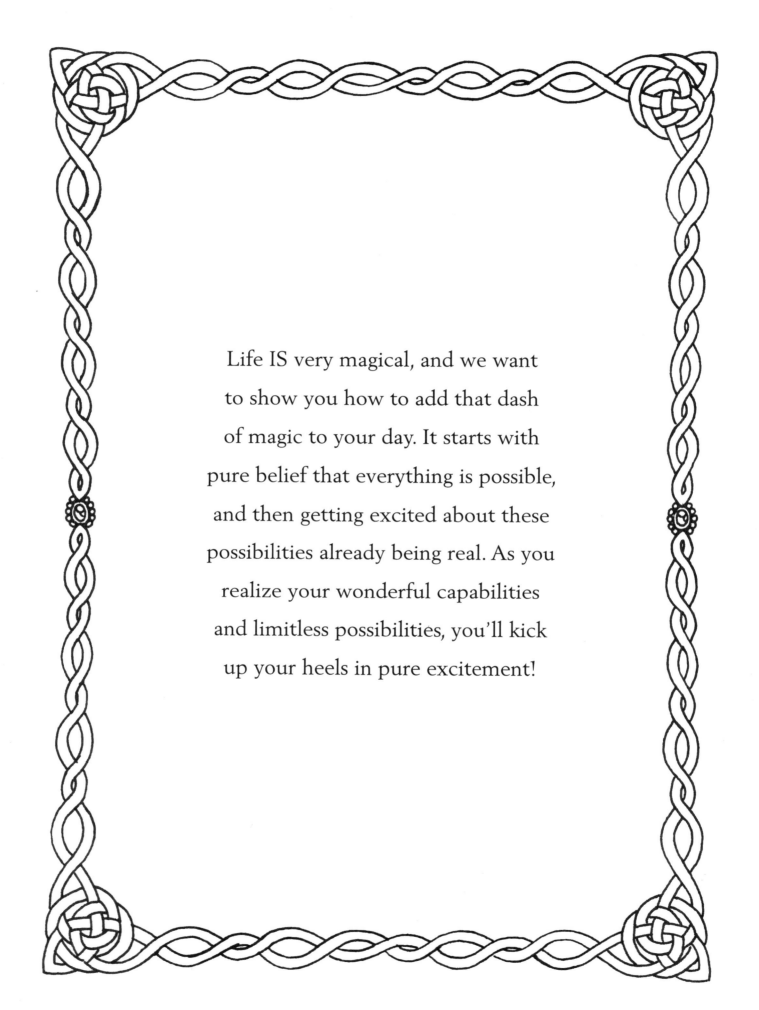

Life IS very magical, and we want
to show you how to add that dash
of magic to your day. It starts with
pure belief that everything is possible,
and then getting excited about these
possibilities already being real. As you
realize your wonderful capabilities
and limitless possibilities, you'll kick
up your heels in pure excitement!

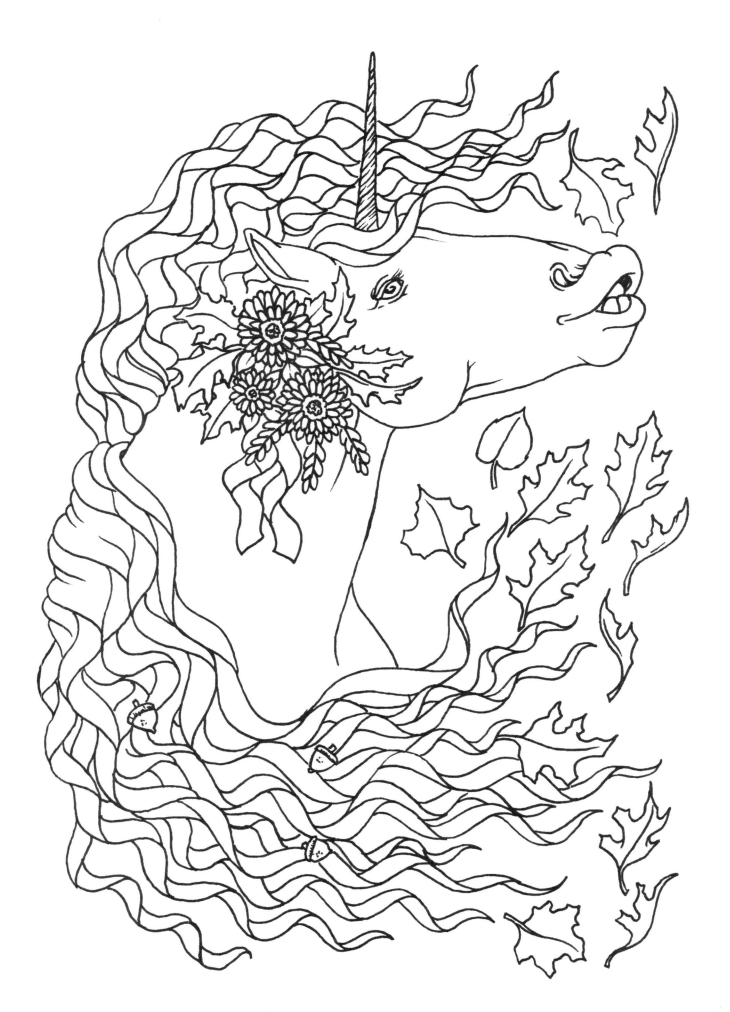

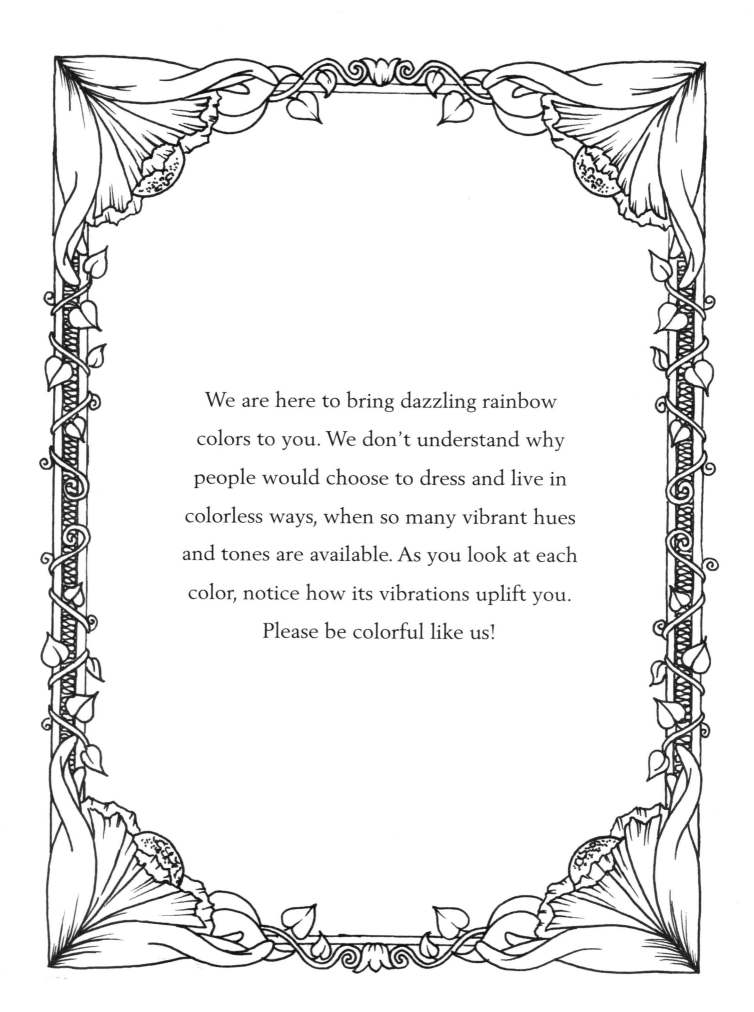

We are here to bring dazzling rainbow colors to you. We don't understand why people would choose to dress and live in colorless ways, when so many vibrant hues and tones are available. As you look at each color, notice how its vibrations uplift you. Please be colorful like us!

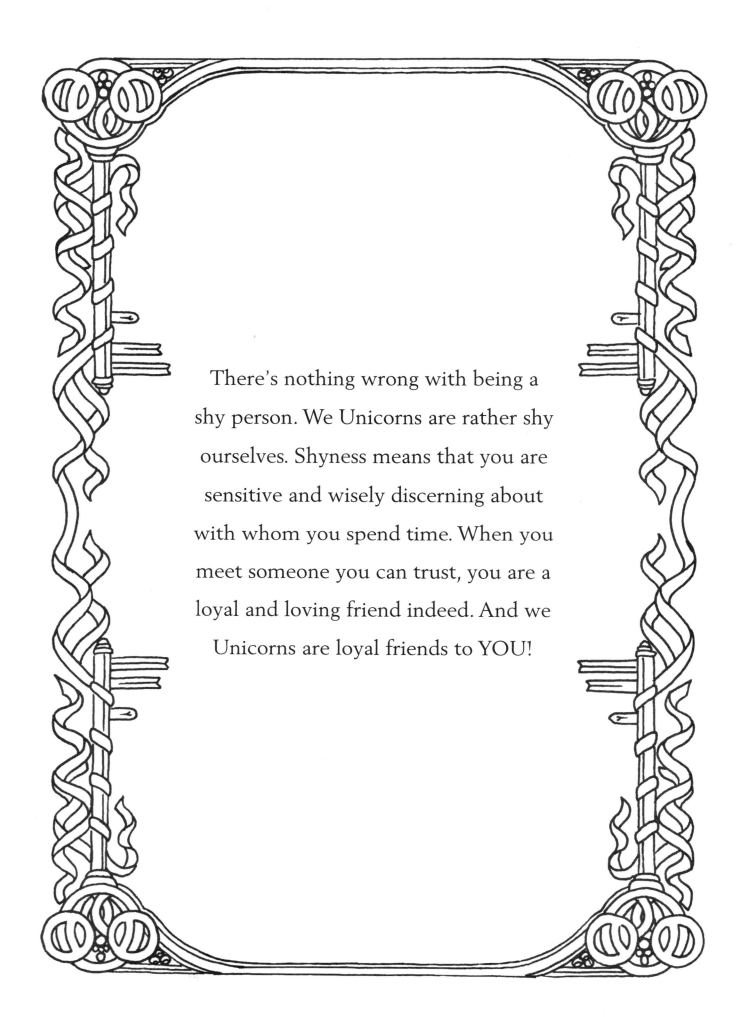

There's nothing wrong with being a shy person. We Unicorns are rather shy ourselves. Shyness means that you are sensitive and wisely discerning about with whom you spend time. When you meet someone you can trust, you are a loyal and loving friend indeed. And we Unicorns are loyal friends to YOU!

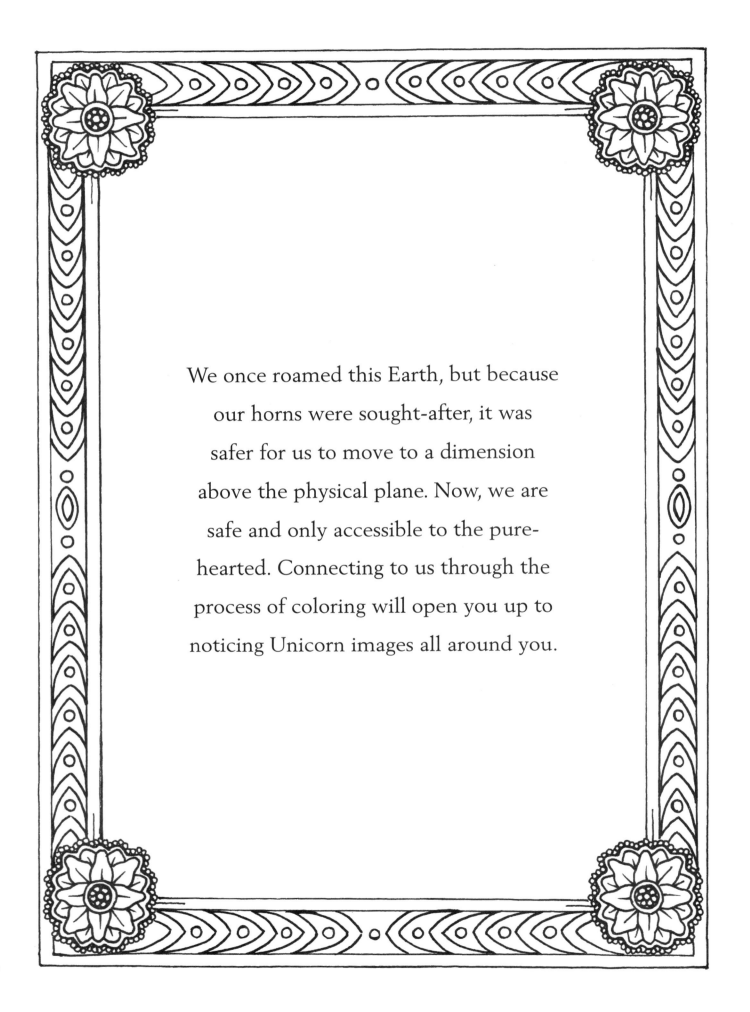

We once roamed this Earth, but because our horns were sought-after, it was safer for us to move to a dimension above the physical plane. Now, we are safe and only accessible to the pure-hearted. Connecting to us through the process of coloring will open you up to noticing Unicorn images all around you.

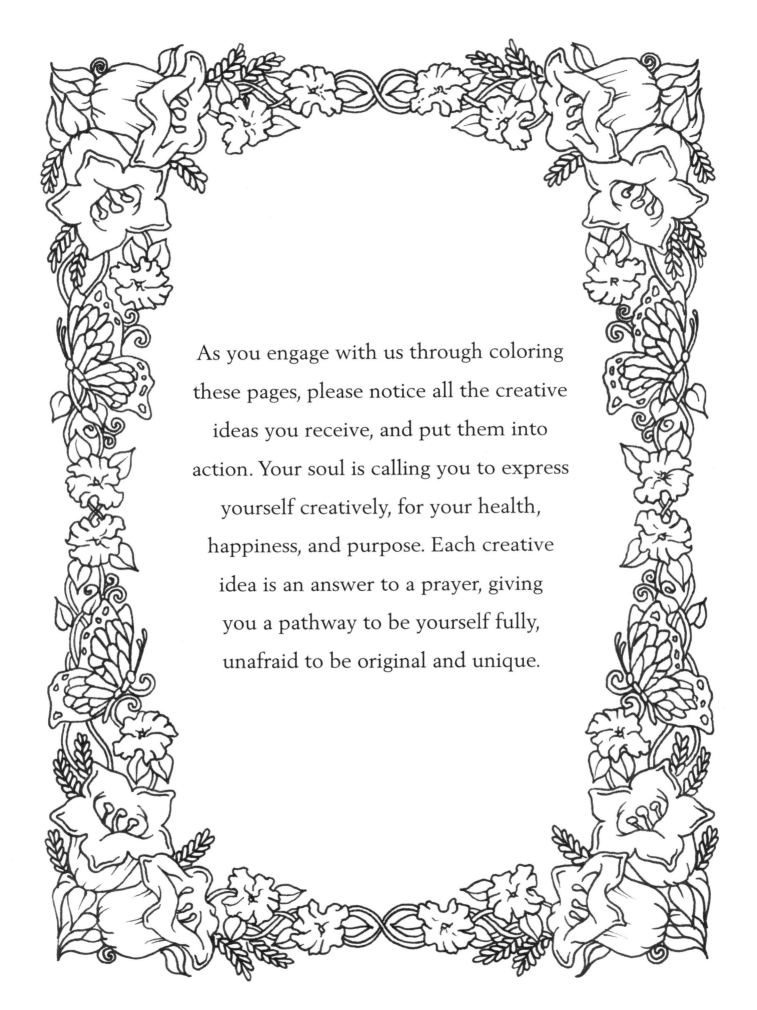

As you engage with us through coloring these pages, please notice all the creative ideas you receive, and put them into action. Your soul is calling you to express yourself creatively, for your health, happiness, and purpose. Each creative idea is an answer to a prayer, giving you a pathway to be yourself fully, unafraid to be original and unique.

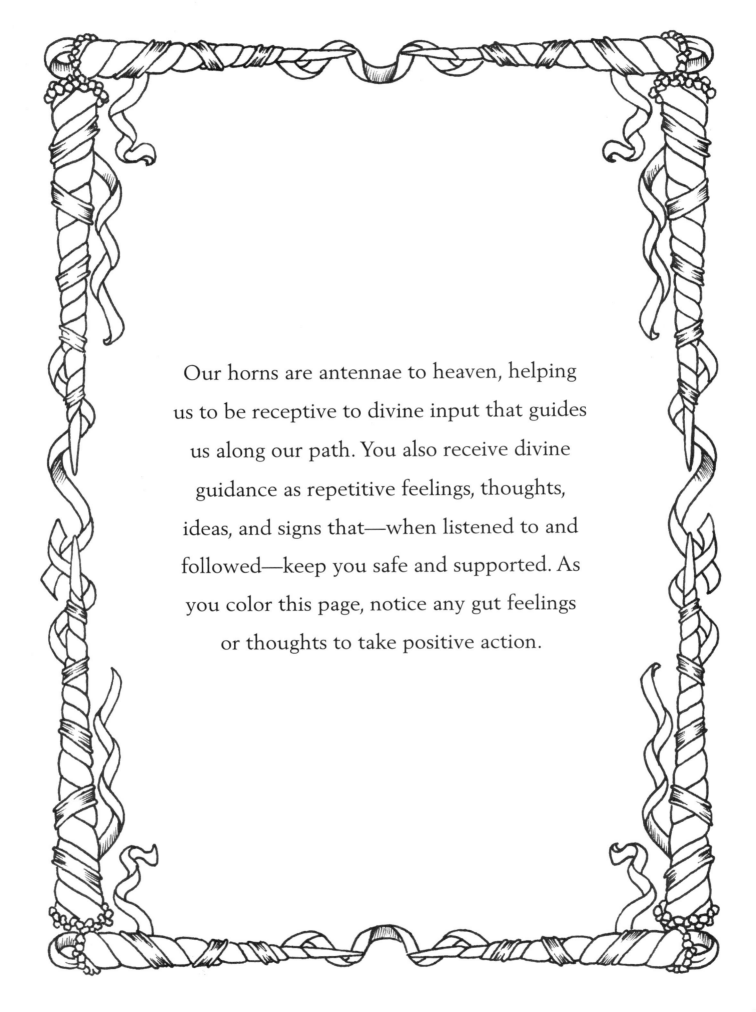

Our horns are antennae to heaven, helping us to be receptive to divine input that guides us along our path. You also receive divine guidance as repetitive feelings, thoughts, ideas, and signs that—when listened to and followed—keep you safe and supported. As you color this page, notice any gut feelings or thoughts to take positive action.

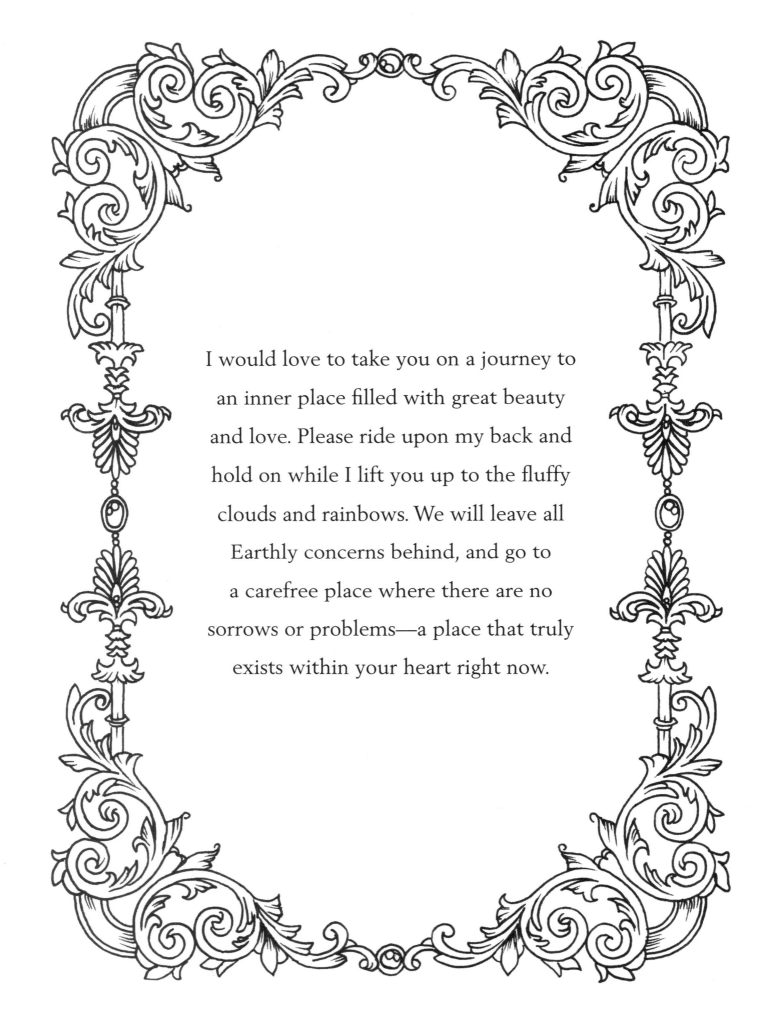

I would love to take you on a journey to
an inner place filled with great beauty
and love. Please ride upon my back and
hold on while I lift you up to the fluffy
clouds and rainbows. We will leave all
Earthly concerns behind, and go to
a carefree place where there are no
sorrows or problems—a place that truly
exists within your heart right now.

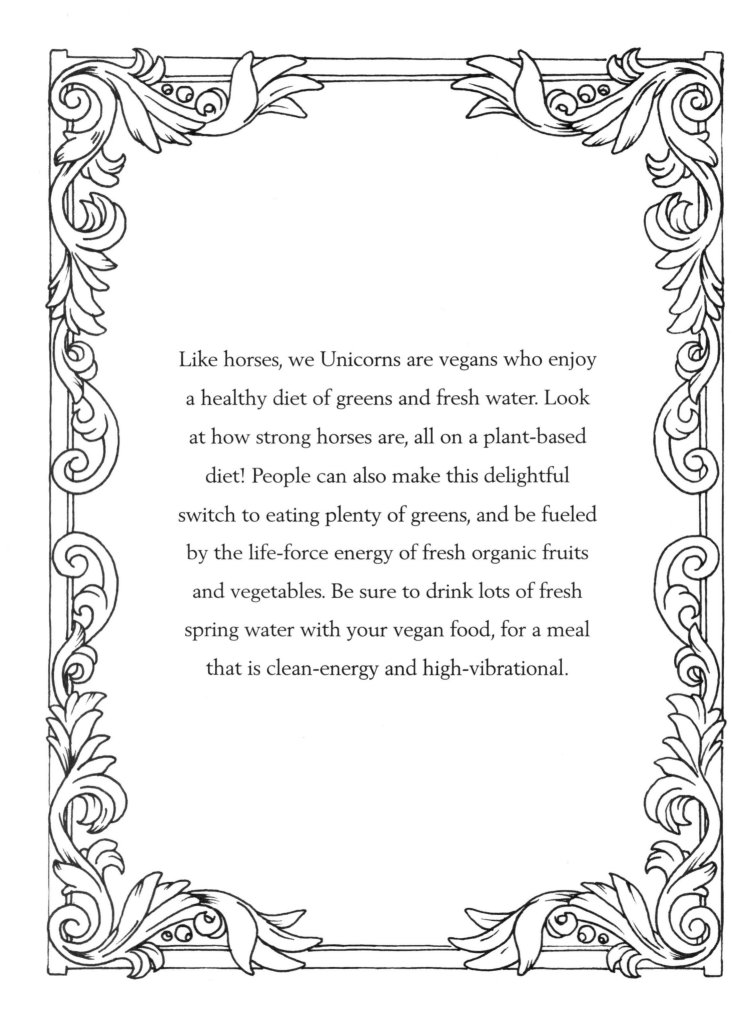

Like horses, we Unicorns are vegans who enjoy a healthy diet of greens and fresh water. Look at how strong horses are, all on a plant-based diet! People can also make this delightful switch to eating plenty of greens, and be fueled by the life-force energy of fresh organic fruits and vegetables. Be sure to drink lots of fresh spring water with your vegan food, for a meal that is clean-energy and high-vibrational.

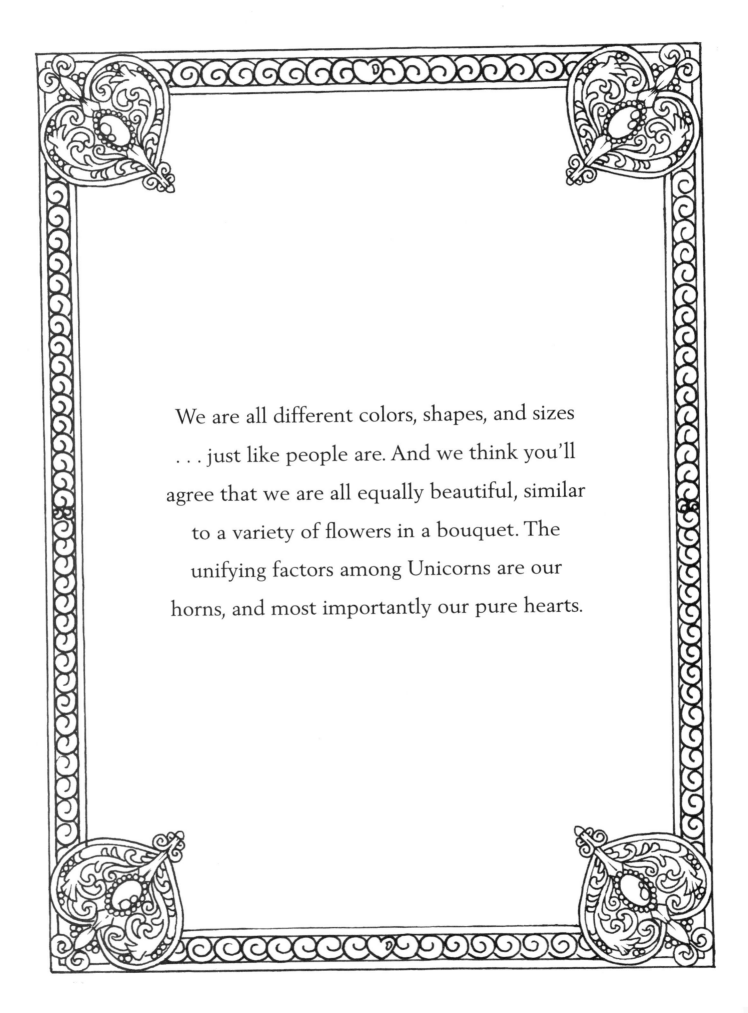

We are all different colors, shapes, and sizes
. . . just like people are. And we think you'll
agree that we are all equally beautiful, similar
to a variety of flowers in a bouquet. The
unifying factors among Unicorns are our
horns, and most importantly our pure hearts.

What do you dream of? There's an
alternative reality that we can enter together,
where dreams are born in beautiful, bold
colors. This rainbow-colored path is filled
with happy, joyful feelings. Together,
we can kick up our heels in delight at
the endless possibilities awaiting us!

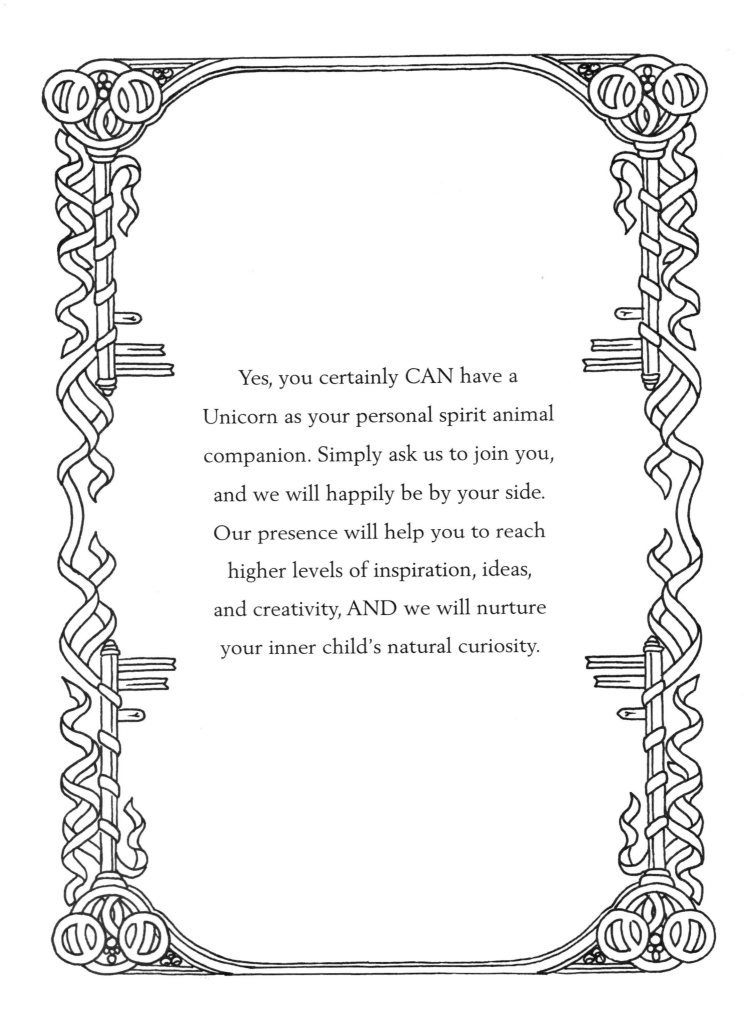

Yes, you certainly CAN have a
Unicorn as your personal spirit animal
companion. Simply ask us to join you,
and we will happily be by your side.
Our presence will help you to reach
higher levels of inspiration, ideas,
and creativity, AND we will nurture
your inner child's natural curiosity.

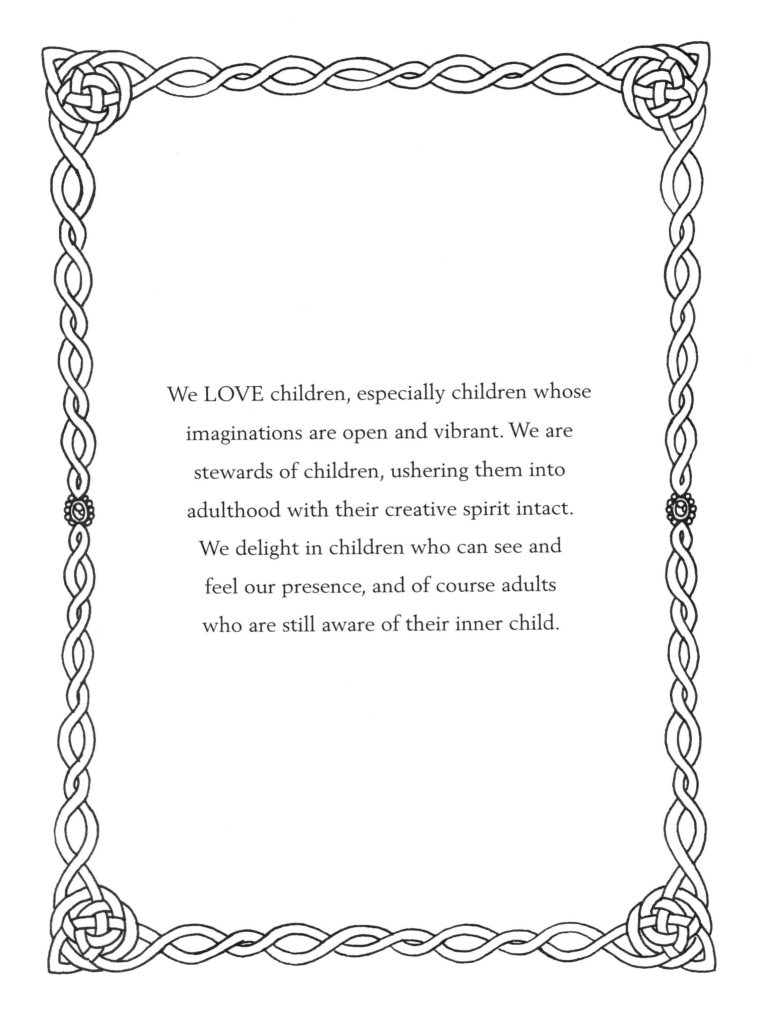

We LOVE children, especially children whose
imaginations are open and vibrant. We are
stewards of children, ushering them into
adulthood with their creative spirit intact.
We delight in children who can see and
feel our presence, and of course adults
who are still aware of their inner child.

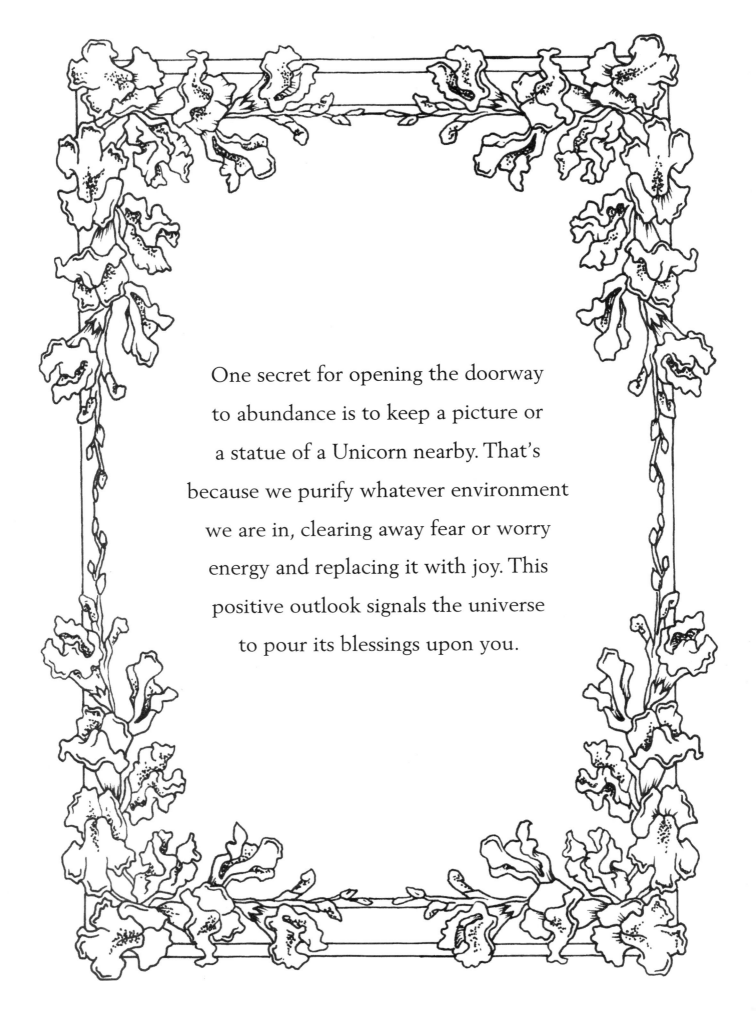

One secret for opening the doorway
to abundance is to keep a picture or
a statue of a Unicorn nearby. That's
because we purify whatever environment
we are in, clearing away fear or worry
energy and replacing it with joy. This
positive outlook signals the universe
to pour its blessings upon you.

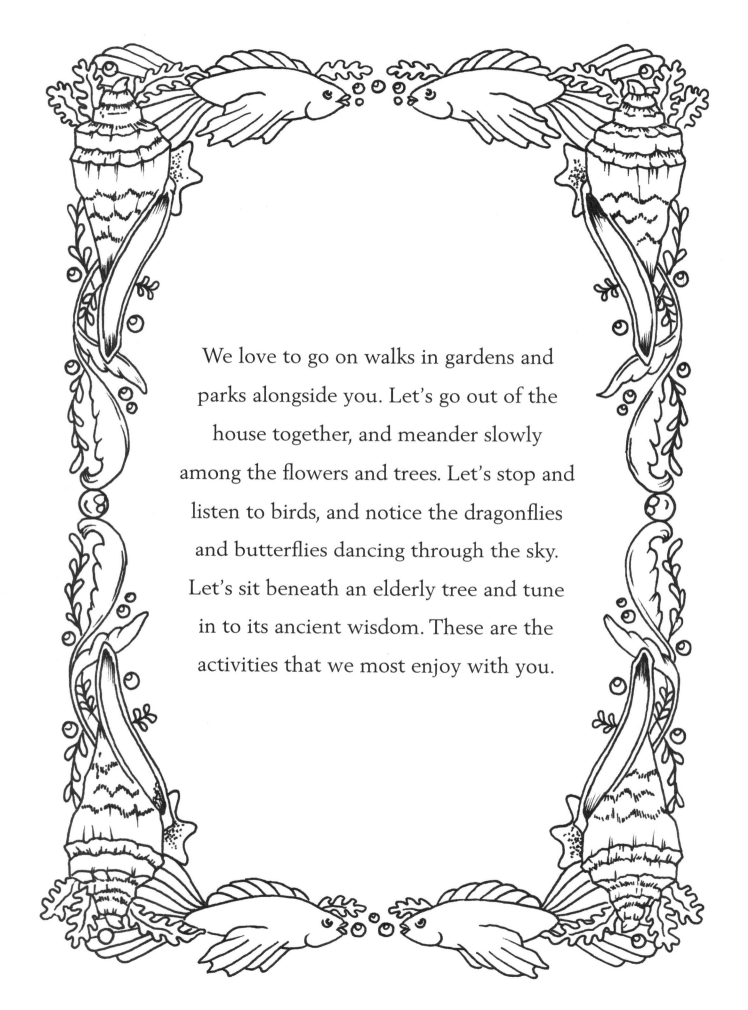

We love to go on walks in gardens and parks alongside you. Let's go out of the house together, and meander slowly among the flowers and trees. Let's stop and listen to birds, and notice the dragonflies and butterflies dancing through the sky. Let's sit beneath an elderly tree and tune in to its ancient wisdom. These are the activities that we most enjoy with you.

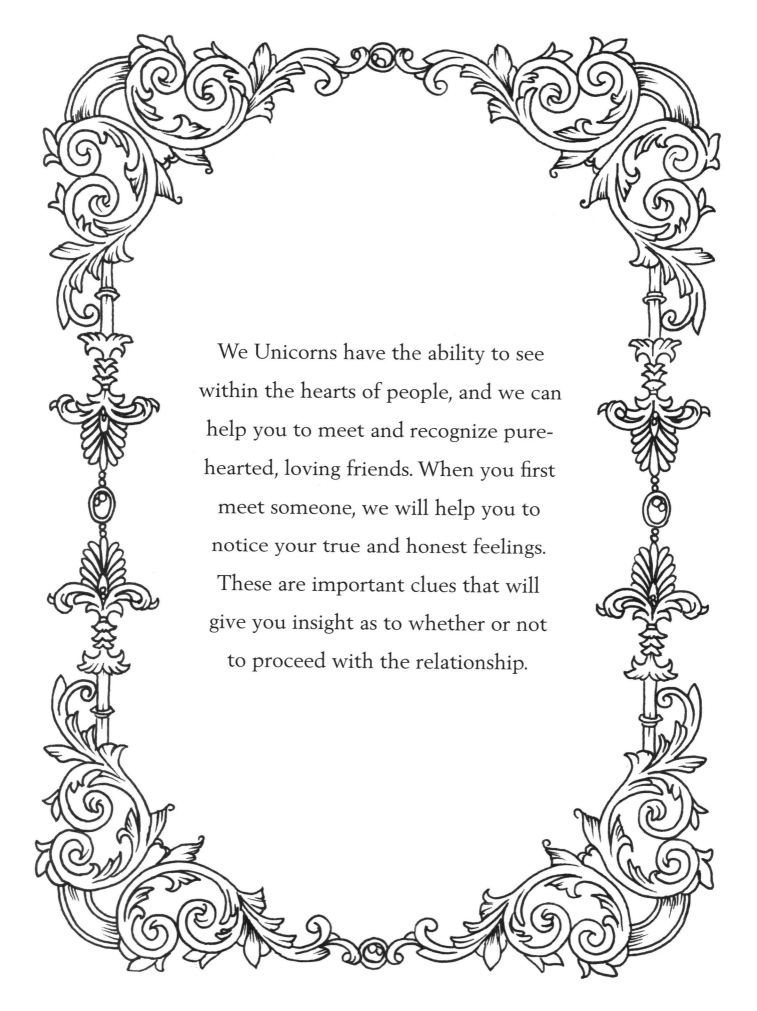

We Unicorns have the ability to see within the hearts of people, and we can help you to meet and recognize pure-hearted, loving friends. When you first meet someone, we will help you to notice your true and honest feelings. These are important clues that will give you insight as to whether or not to proceed with the relationship.

There is strength in being a sweet, kind, and sensitive being—and yet there are also some challenges. We have been on this Earth for thousands of years. As ancient beings, we have realized that the best way to deal with problems is to face them without fear, do what we can—and then let them go.

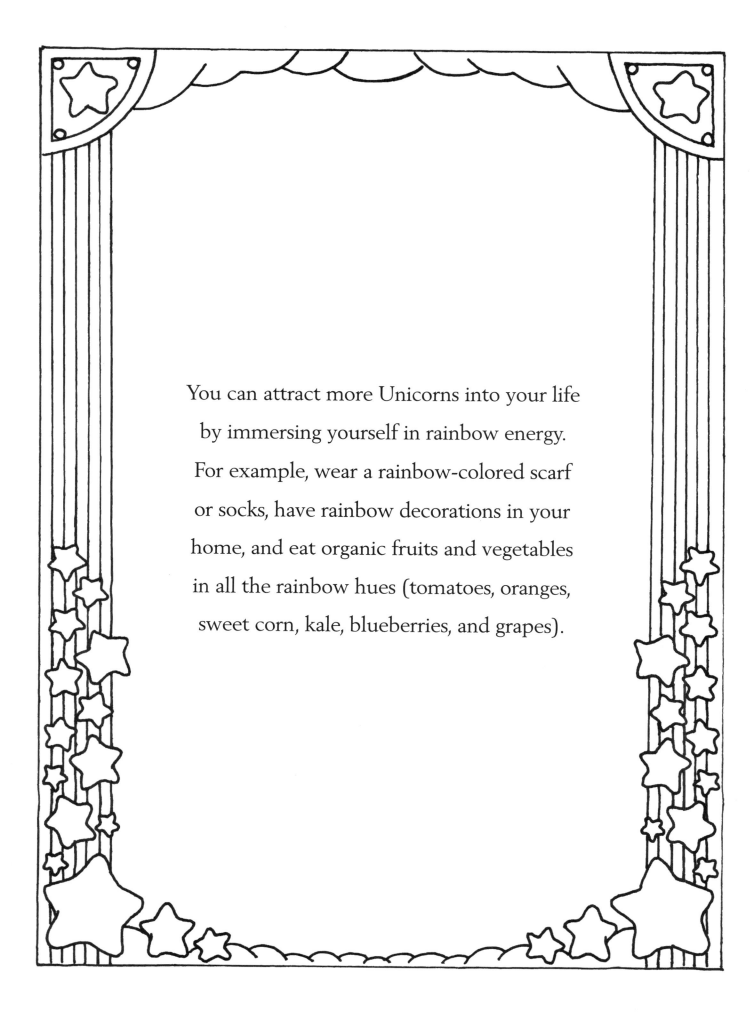

You can attract more Unicorns into your life
by immersing yourself in rainbow energy.
For example, wear a rainbow-colored scarf
or socks, have rainbow decorations in your
home, and eat organic fruits and vegetables
in all the rainbow hues (tomatoes, oranges,
sweet corn, kale, blueberries, and grapes).

We are so much more than horses
with horns upon our heads! We have
worked diligently to become the highest
vibrational and purest examples of beings
who have their hearts completely open
to compassion and unconditional love.
Being in our presence by coloring these
images, and surrounding yourself with
images of Unicorns, automatically uplifts
your outlook and opens your heart.

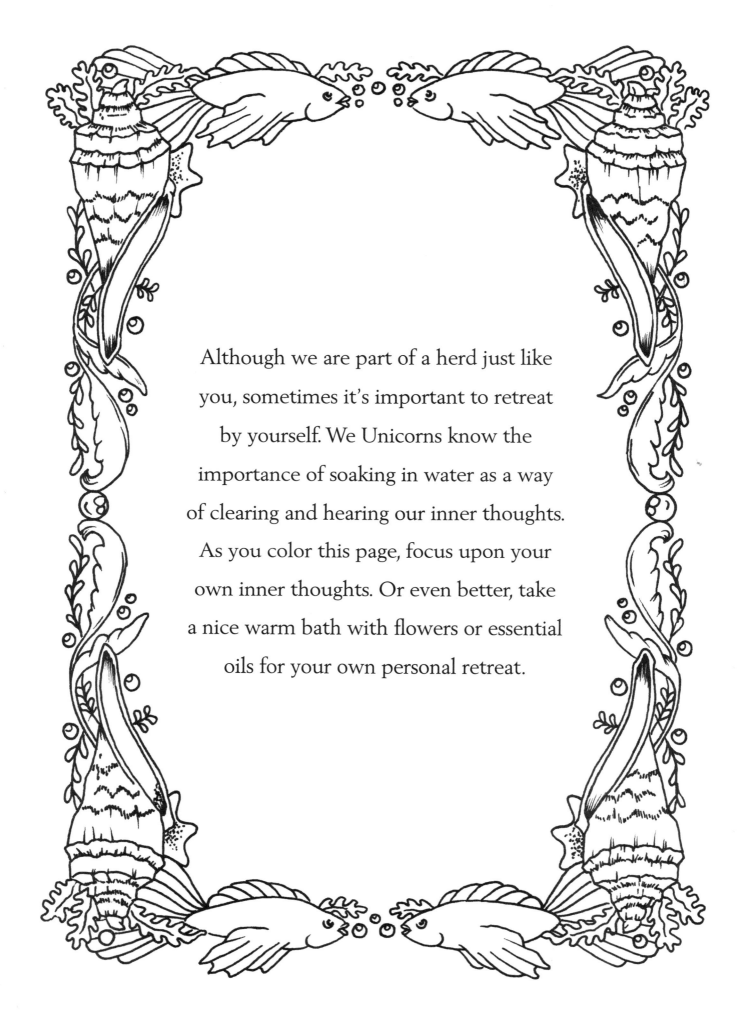

Although we are part of a herd just like you, sometimes it's important to retreat by yourself. We Unicorns know the importance of soaking in water as a way of clearing and hearing our inner thoughts. As you color this page, focus upon your own inner thoughts. Or even better, take a nice warm bath with flowers or essential oils for your own personal retreat.

Playtime is an important responsibility
to yourself, as playing helps you to relax,
discharge energy, and enjoy yourself.
Sometimes you may enjoy playing by
yourself, and at other times you share fun
and laughter with your herd of friends
and family. Be sure to balance all the work
you are doing with plenty of playtime.

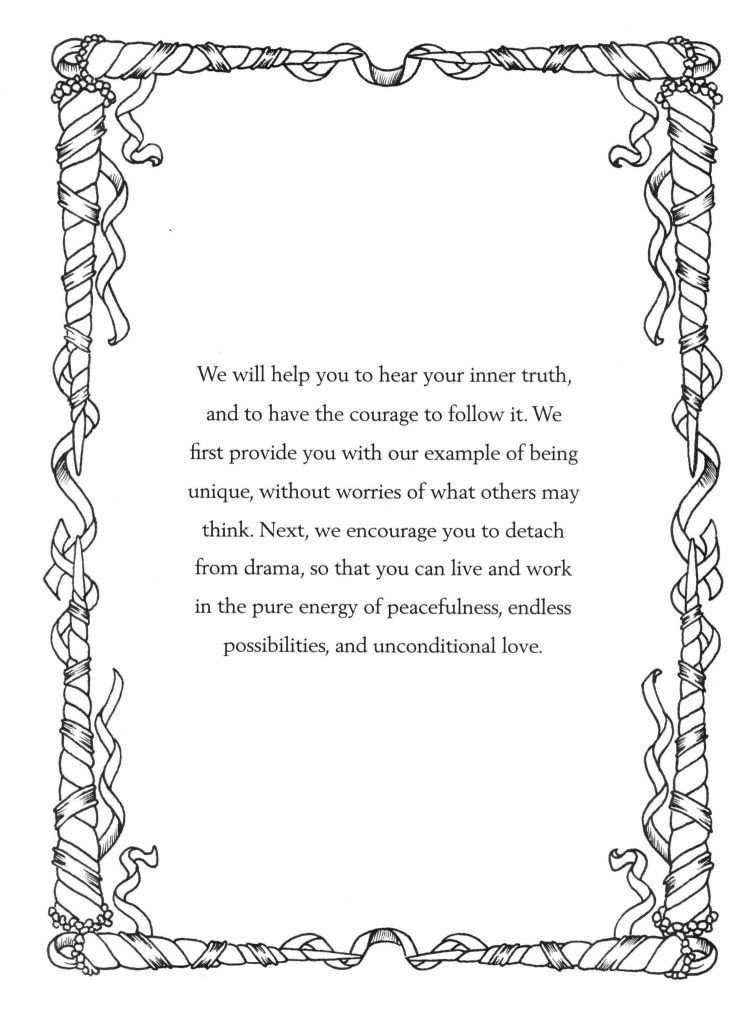

We will help you to hear your inner truth, and to have the courage to follow it. We first provide you with our example of being unique, without worries of what others may think. Next, we encourage you to detach from drama, so that you can live and work in the pure energy of peacefulness, endless possibilities, and unconditional love.

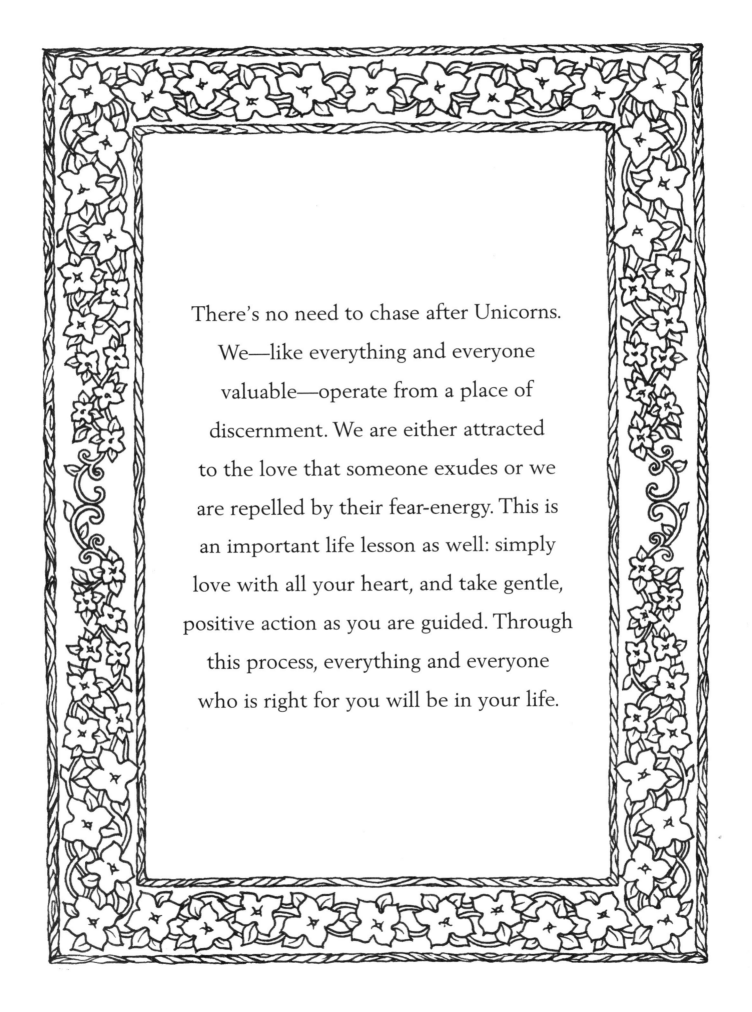

There's no need to chase after Unicorns.
We—like everything and everyone
valuable—operate from a place of
discernment. We are either attracted
to the love that someone exudes or we
are repelled by their fear-energy. This is
an important life lesson as well: simply
love with all your heart, and take gentle,
positive action as you are guided. Through
this process, everything and everyone
who is right for you will be in your life.

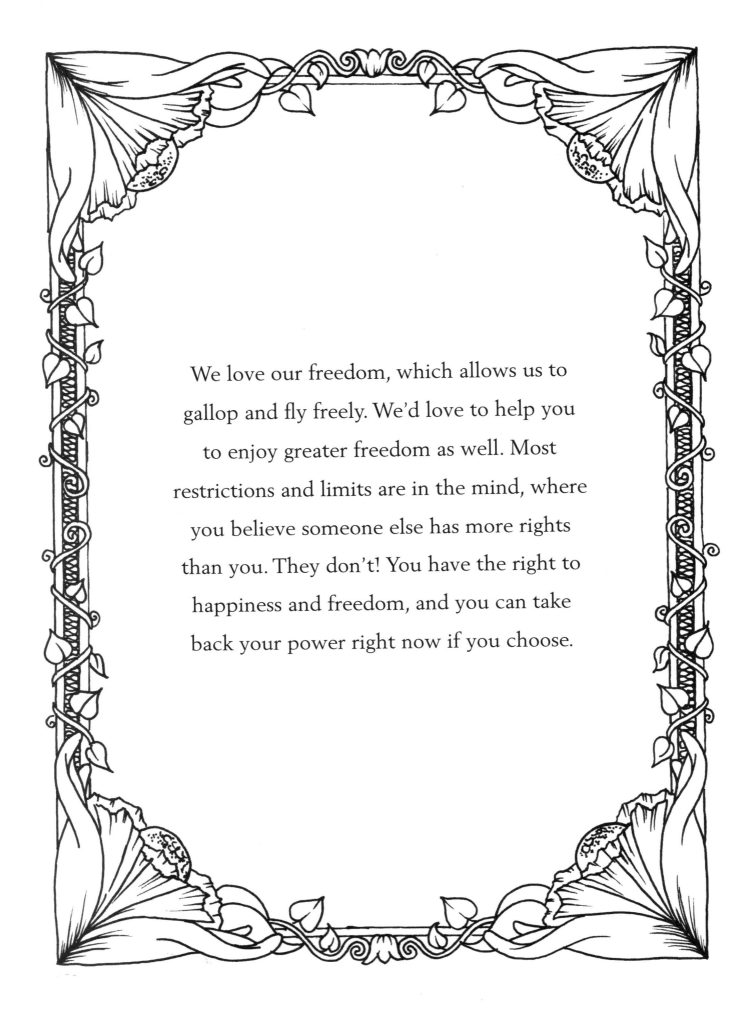

We love our freedom, which allows us to gallop and fly freely. We'd love to help you to enjoy greater freedom as well. Most restrictions and limits are in the mind, where you believe someone else has more rights than you. They don't! You have the right to happiness and freedom, and you can take back your power right now if you choose.

Perhaps lately you've been questioning
your path or beliefs, which is a part
of the spiritual journey that everyone
goes through. Like a lily opening her
petals to the daylight, you are noticing
which spiritual beliefs help you to feel
at peace. The spiritual path that is right
for you will help you to keep your
heart open to love and happiness. As
we Unicorns do, always choose a path
paved in pure and unconditional love.

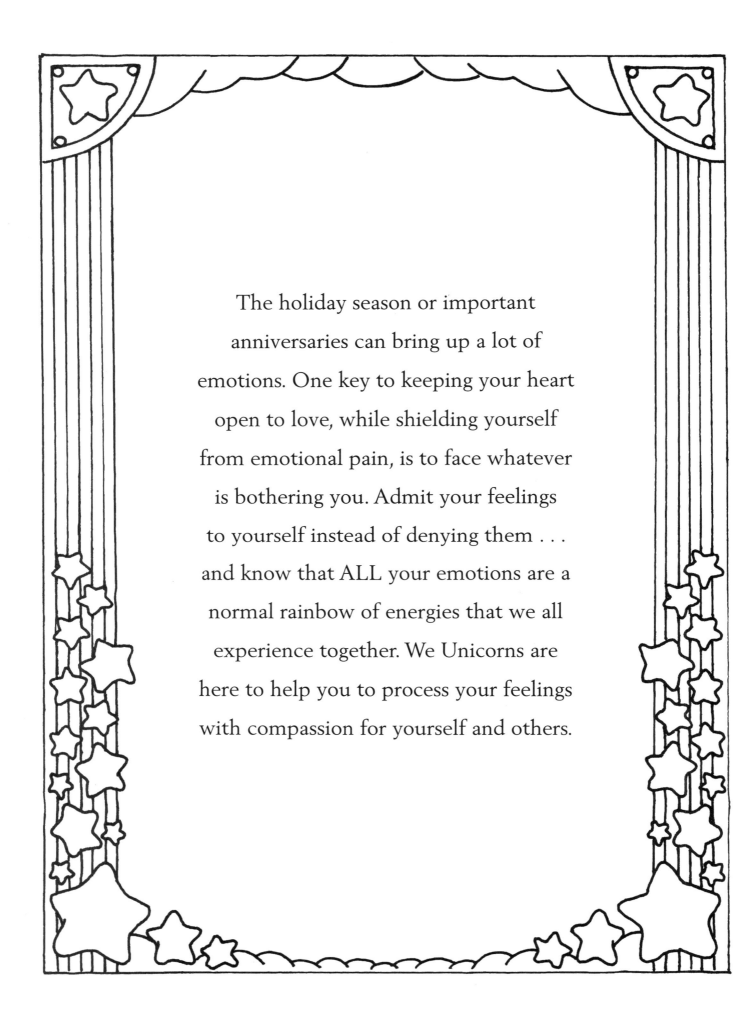

The holiday season or important
anniversaries can bring up a lot of
emotions. One key to keeping your heart
open to love, while shielding yourself
from emotional pain, is to face whatever
is bothering you. Admit your feelings
to yourself instead of denying them . . .
and know that ALL your emotions are a
normal rainbow of energies that we all
experience together. We Unicorns are
here to help you to process your feelings
with compassion for yourself and others.

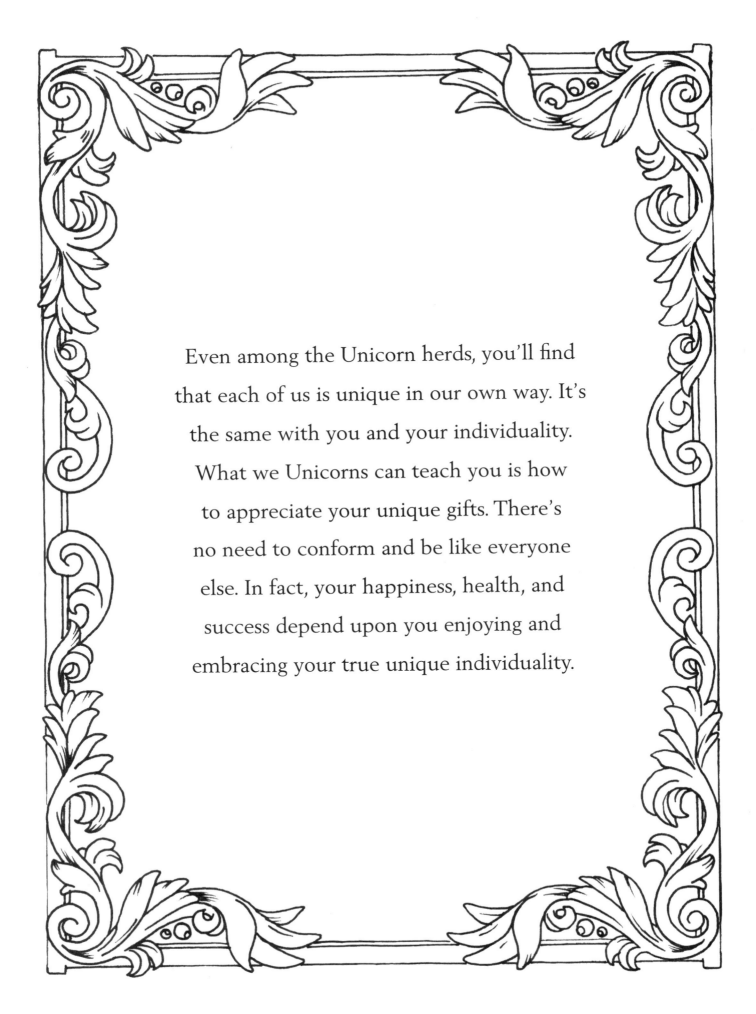

Even among the Unicorn herds, you'll find
that each of us is unique in our own way. It's
the same with you and your individuality.
What we Unicorns can teach you is how
to appreciate your unique gifts. There's
no need to conform and be like everyone
else. In fact, your happiness, health, and
success depend upon you enjoying and
embracing your true unique individuality.

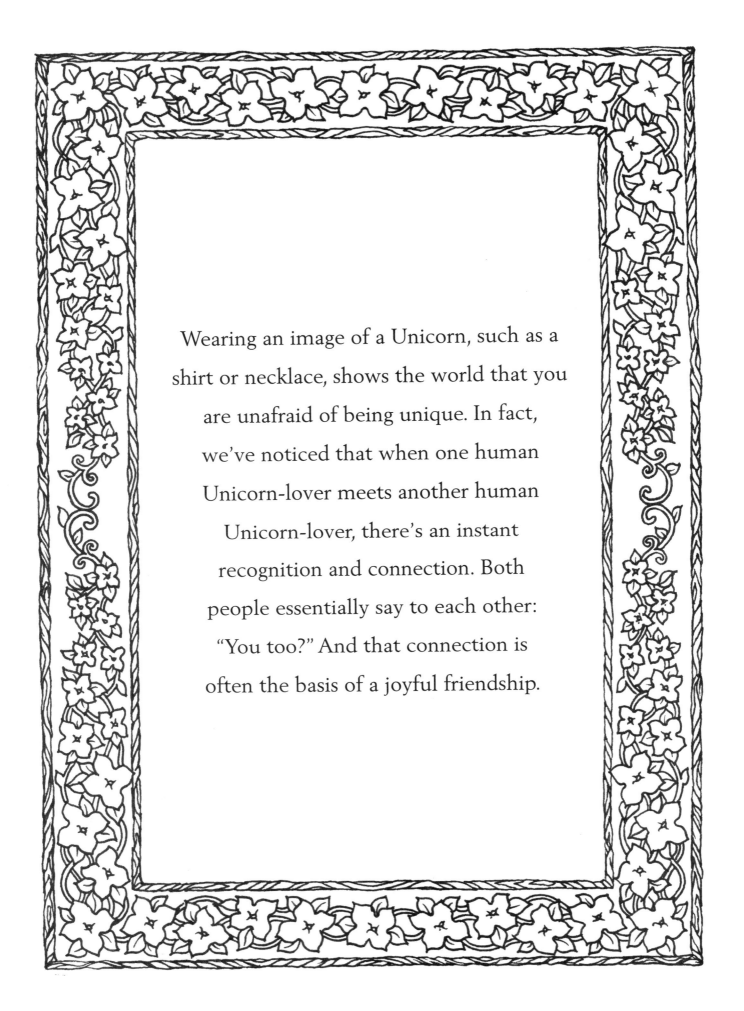

Wearing an image of a Unicorn, such as a shirt or necklace, shows the world that you are unafraid of being unique. In fact, we've noticed that when one human Unicorn-lover meets another human Unicorn-lover, there's an instant recognition and connection. Both people essentially say to each other: "You too?" And that connection is often the basis of a joyful friendship.

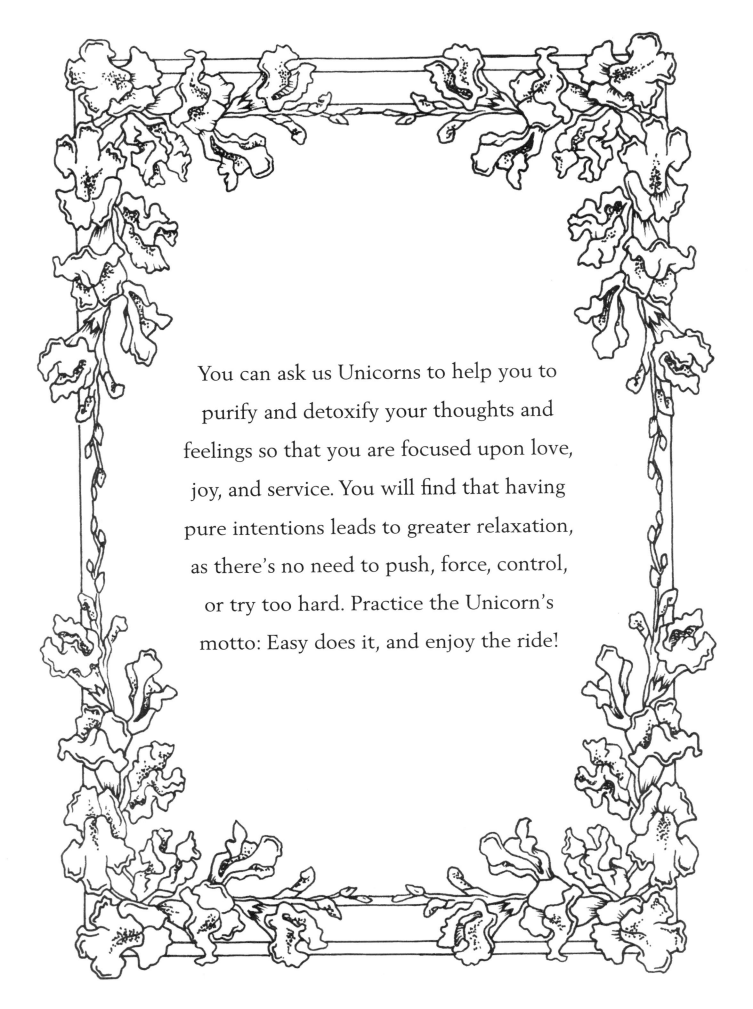

You can ask us Unicorns to help you to purify and detoxify your thoughts and feelings so that you are focused upon love, joy, and service. You will find that having pure intentions leads to greater relaxation, as there's no need to push, force, control, or try too hard. Practice the Unicorn's motto: Easy does it, and enjoy the ride!

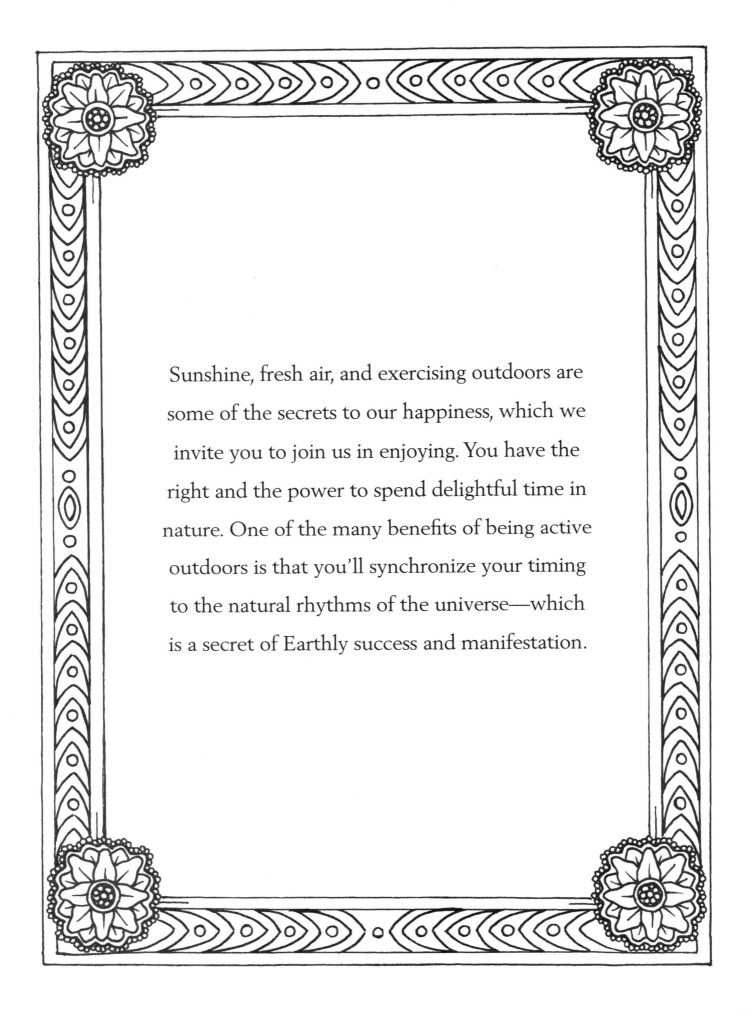

Sunshine, fresh air, and exercising outdoors are some of the secrets to our happiness, which we invite you to join us in enjoying. You have the right and the power to spend delightful time in nature. One of the many benefits of being active outdoors is that you'll synchronize your timing to the natural rhythms of the universe—which is a secret of Earthly success and manifestation.

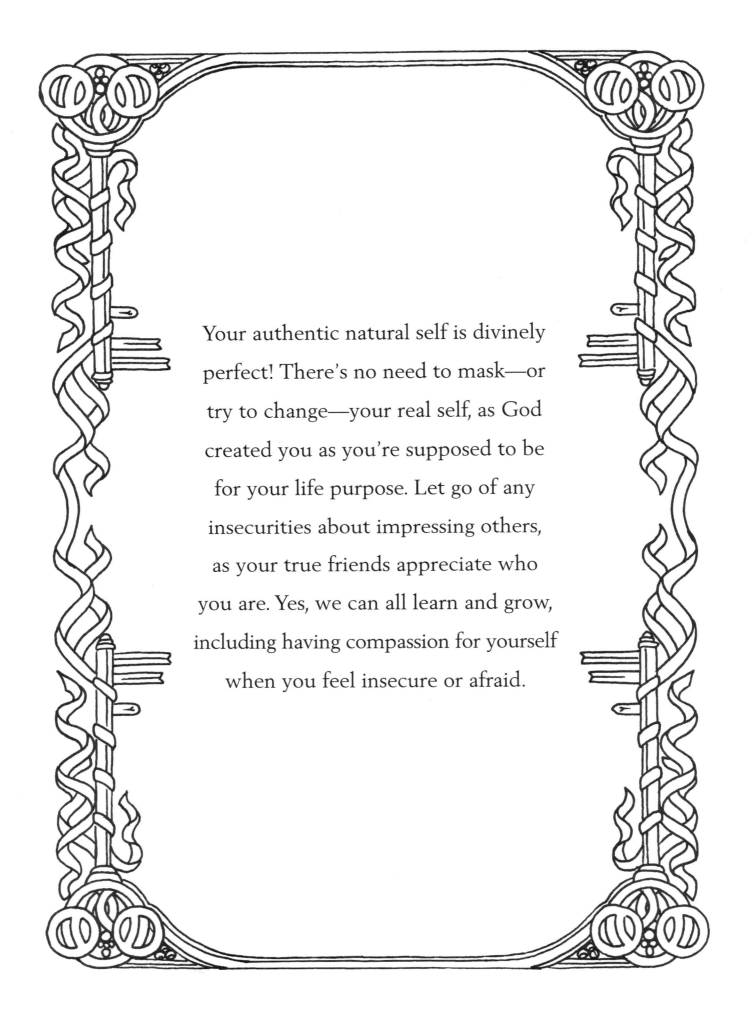

Your authentic natural self is divinely
perfect! There's no need to mask—or
try to change—your real self, as God
created you as you're supposed to be
for your life purpose. Let go of any
insecurities about impressing others,
as your true friends appreciate who
you are. Yes, we can all learn and grow,
including having compassion for yourself
when you feel insecure or afraid.

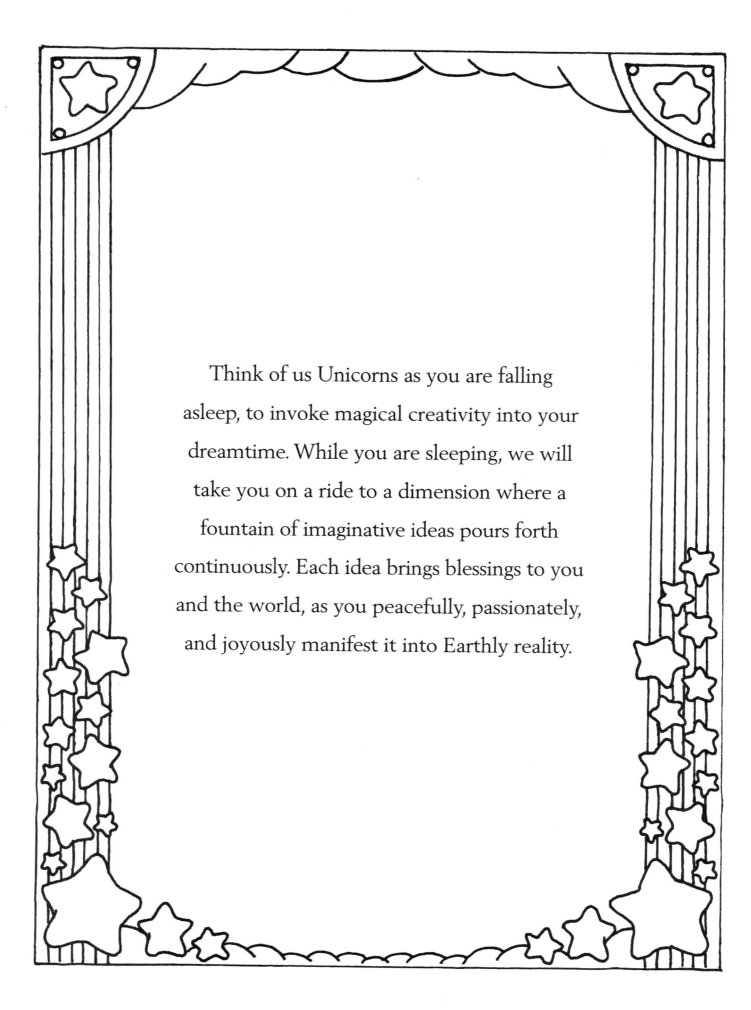

Think of us Unicorns as you are falling asleep, to invoke magical creativity into your dreamtime. While you are sleeping, we will take you on a ride to a dimension where a fountain of imaginative ideas pours forth continuously. Each idea brings blessings to you and the world, as you peacefully, passionately, and joyously manifest it into Earthly reality.

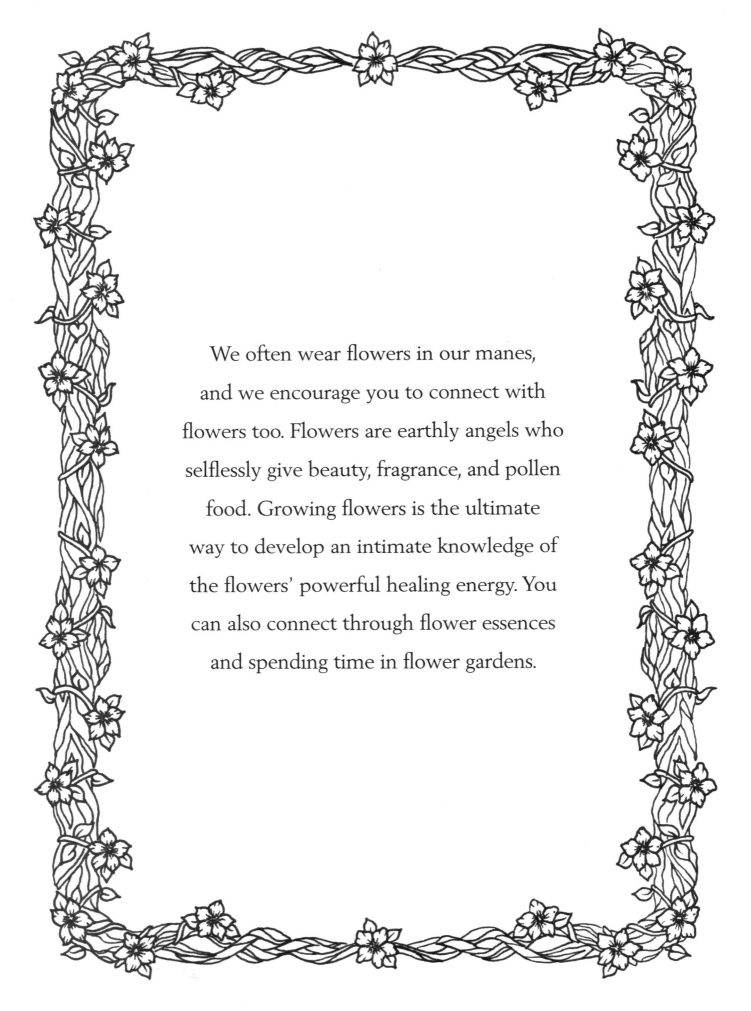

We often wear flowers in our manes,
and we encourage you to connect with
flowers too. Flowers are earthly angels who
selflessly give beauty, fragrance, and pollen
food. Growing flowers is the ultimate
way to develop an intimate knowledge of
the flowers' powerful healing energy. You
can also connect through flower essences
and spending time in flower gardens.

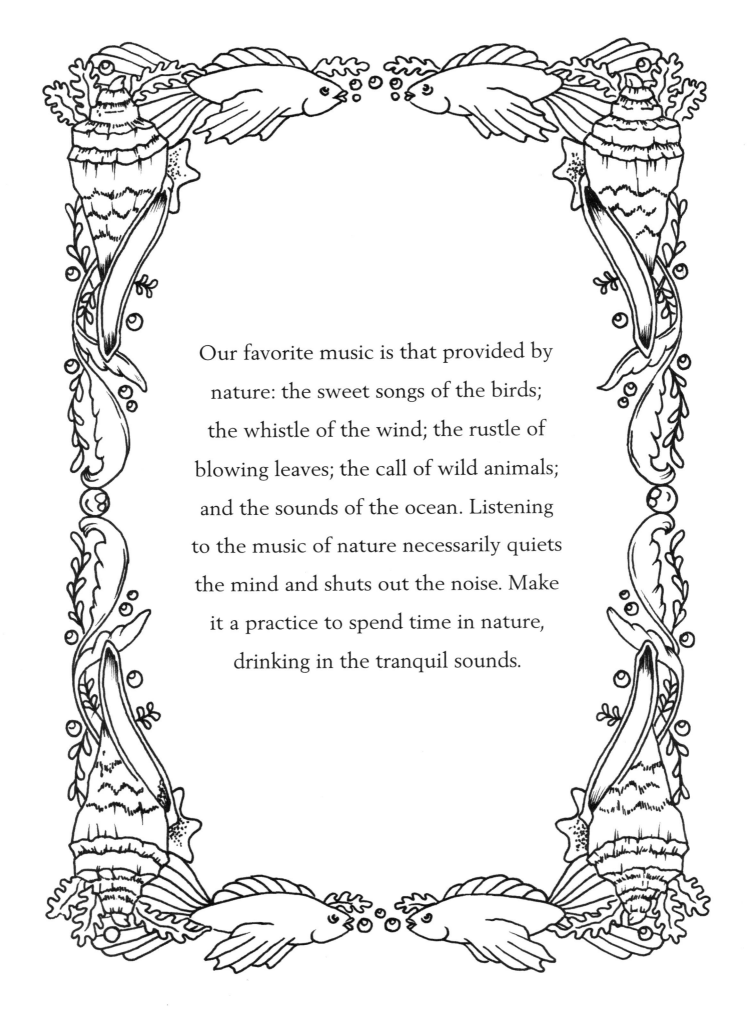

Our favorite music is that provided by nature: the sweet songs of the birds; the whistle of the wind; the rustle of blowing leaves; the call of wild animals; and the sounds of the ocean. Listening to the music of nature necessarily quiets the mind and shuts out the noise. Make it a practice to spend time in nature, drinking in the tranquil sounds.

Just like you, we Unicorns give all glory to God for creating us from pure, unconditional love. The more we focus upon love, the more love we experience and receive. Each time that you or I accept and give love, we are honoring God's mission to create a world of peace, love, harmony . . . and rainbows!

If you were a Unicorn, what would your name be? Let's think of one together right now. First, think of your favorite color. That's your Unicorn first name. Next, what is your favorite flower? That's your Unicorn middle name. And then think of your favorite crystal. That's your Unicorn last name. Put them all together, and there's your Unicorn name. How do you like it? (You can always change any part of your name whenever you'd like).

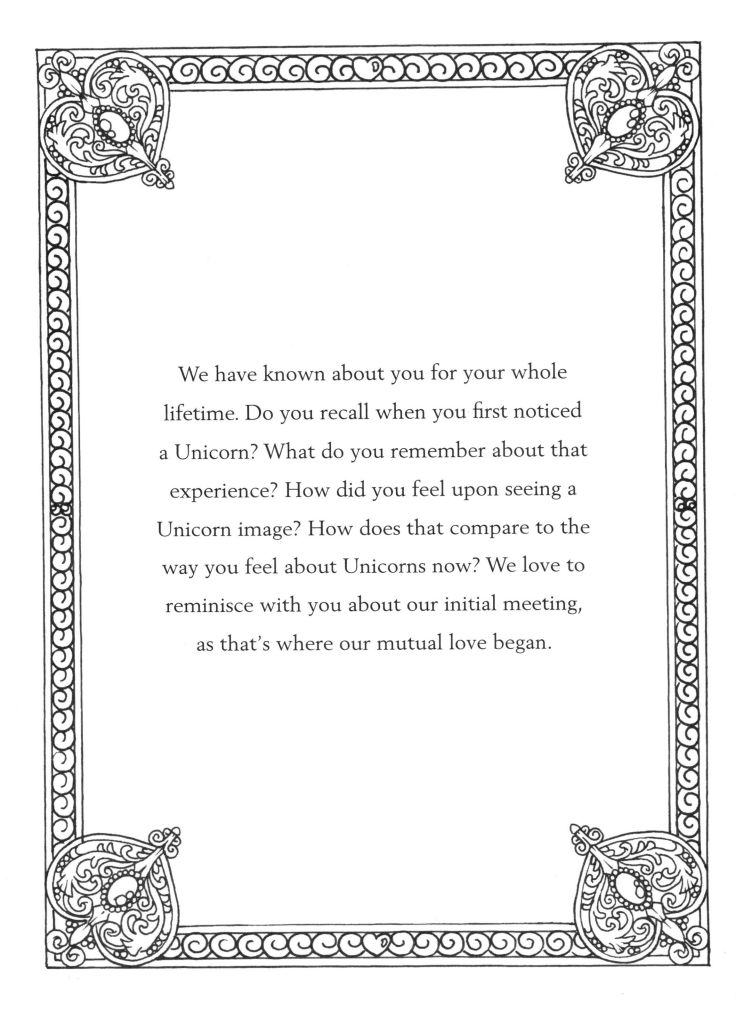

We have known about you for your whole lifetime. Do you recall when you first noticed a Unicorn? What do you remember about that experience? How did you feel upon seeing a Unicorn image? How does that compare to the way you feel about Unicorns now? We love to reminisce with you about our initial meeting, as that's where our mutual love began.

About the Author

Doreen Virtue holds B.A., M.A., and Ph.D. degrees in counseling psychology. She's the author of more than 50 books and oracle card decks dealing with spiritual topics. Best known for her work with the angels, Doreen is frequently called "The Angel Lady."

A lifelong activist and a vegan since 1996, Doreen is involved in charities and movements that support a healthy environment, fair treatment of animals, clean air and water, and organic non-GMO food for all.

Doreen has appeared on *Oprah*, CNN, and other television and radio programs, and writes the weekly column "My Guardian Angel" for *Woman's World* magazine. Her products are available in most languages worldwide, on Kindle and other e-book platforms, and as iTunes apps. She also has a live weekly radio show on HayHouseRadio.com.

www.angeltherapy.com

About the Illustrator

Heather Luciana grew up in the suburbs of New Jersey, just outside New York City. She has been drawing since the age of six, and is primarily self-taught. During her school years she took many art classes to hone her skills and learn new techniques.

Heather's main areas of interest are horses and the fantasy genre, and her trademark style features strong outlines and vibrant colors. Her preferred media are watercolor, colored pencil, and acrylic.

She adores the chance to express her joy through bringing people's imaginings to life, sharing her art, and encouraging others to be creative.

[f] **DreamSong Designs**

Bonus Content

Thank you for purchasing *Messages from the Unicorns Coloring Book* by Doreen Virtue. This product includes a free download! To access this bonus content, please visit www.hayhouse.com/download and enter the Product ID and Download Code as they appear below:

Product ID: 5289

Download Code: unicorn

For further assistance, please contact Hay House Customer Care by phone: US (800) 654-5126 or INTL CC+(760) 431-7695 or visit www.hayhouse.com/contact.

Thank you again for your Hay House purchase. Enjoy!

Hay House, Inc. • P.O. Box 5100 • Carlsbad, CA 92018 • (800) 654-5126

Caution: This audio program features meditation/visualization exercises that render it inappropriate for use while driving or operating heavy machinery.

Publisher's note: Hay House products are intended to be powerful, inspirational, and life-changing tools for personal growth and healing. They are not intended as a substitute for medical care. Please use this audio program under the supervision of your care provider. Neither the author nor Hay House, Inc., assumes any responsibility for your improper use of this product.

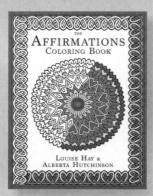

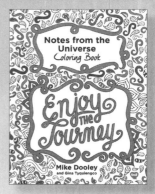